VITAL TO EARTH!
Keystone Species Explained

BEAVERS

IN THEIR ECOSYSTEMS

by Della O'Dowd

BEARPORT
PUBLISHING

Minneapolis, Minnesota

Credits
Cover and title page, © Troy Harrison/Getty Images; 4–5, © Suzi Eszterhas/Minden; 7T, © Gustavo
Enrique Cortez/iStock; 7B, © gluuker/iStock; 8–9, © Rosanne Tackaberry/Alamy; 9, © Mihai__Andritoiu/
Shutterstock; 10–11, © Universal Images Group North America LLC/Alamy; 12–13, © Panoramic Images/
Alamy; 14–15, © Panoramic Images/Alamy; 16, © OceanProd/Adobe Stock; 16–17, © KarenMassier/
iStock; 18–19, © stanley45/iStock; 22–23, © Evgenii Mitroshin/iStock; 24–25, © Ricky Park Scott/Alamy;
26–27, © Cavan Images/Getty Images; 28, © Ilkka/Adobe Stock; 29T, © FatCamera/iStock; 29TM, ©
milehightraveler/iStock; 29M, © PrathanChorruangsak/iStock; 29BM, © SawitreeLyaon/iStock; 29B, ©
FG Trade/iStock.

Bearport Publishing Company Product Development Team
President: Jen Jenson; Director of Product Development: Spencer Brinker; Managing Editor: Allison Juda;
Associate Editor: Naomi Reich; Associate Editor: Tiana Tran; Art Director: Colin O'Dea; Designer: Elena
Klinkner; Designer: Kayla Eggert; Product Development Assistant: Owen Hamlin

STATEMENT ON USAGE OF GENERATIVE ARTIFICIAL INTELLIGENCE
Bearport Publishing remains committed to publishing high-quality nonfiction books. Therefore, we
restrict the use of generative AI to ensure accuracy of all text and visual components pertaining to a
book's subject. See BearportPublishing.com for details.

Library of Congress Cataloging-in-Publication Data

Names: O'Dowd, Della, author.
Title: Beavers in their ecosystems / by Della O'Dowd.
Description: Minneapolis, Minnesota : Bearport Publishing Company, [2024] |
   Series: Vital to Earth! Keystone species explained | Includes
   bibliographical references and index.
Identifiers: LCCN 2023030974 (print) | LCCN 2023030975 (ebook) | ISBN
   9798889166276 (library binding) | ISBN 9798889166344 (paperback) | ISBN
   9798889166405 (ebook)
Subjects: LCSH: Beavers--Juvenile literature.
Classification: LCC QL737.R632 O86 2024 (print) | LCC QL737.R632 (ebook)
   | DDC 599.37--dc23/eng/20230714
LC record available at https://lccn.loc.gov/2023030974
LC ebook record available at https://lccn.loc.gov/2023030975

For more information, write to Bearport Publishing, 5357 Penn Avenue South, Minneapolis, MN 55419.a

Contents

Beavers at Work

A slow stream flows into a pond that is brimming with life. Fish swim through the calm, clean waters. Many green trees, plants, and grasses grow along the water's edge, offering food and shelter to birds, bugs, turtles, and ducks that live throughout the **wetland**.

Two furry animals with big, flat tails swim out of a large pile of branches in the middle of the water. What are these little creatures? They are beavers, and they are the ones that built this wetland! These hard-working animals are vital to their **ecosystem**.

Beavers build **dams**. These piles of wood, mud, and stones force some stream water onto dry land, creating ponds and lakes that support a lot of plant and animal life.

A Key Animal

Busy pond-building beavers are a keystone **species**—a kind of plant or animal that is crucial to supporting an entire community of plant and animal life within an area. These species shape the land or help balance the populations of plants and animals in a way that benefits everything in the environment.

When beavers are removed from the wetlands they helped create, their dams fall apart and ponds dry up. The wetland plants die off, along with many of the animals, birds, and fish that rely on them. Without beavers, these wetlands can't survive.

Many plants and animals rely on watery wetland homes for at least part of their lives. About half of all **endangered** and threatened animals in North America can be found in wetlands.

Dam Builders

Beavers live near streams and rivers because they spend much of their time chomping on the bark, roots, stems, and leaves of trees that grow alongside them. But this water is often shallow and moves quickly. Beavers prefer deeper, slower water. So, they get busy.

Beavers use tree branches and river mud to build dams to stop the water. As the stream or river slows, water begins to collect, becoming deeper and spreading onto some dry land. This forms a pool of water called a beaver pond.

Algae, moss, water lilies, pondweed, and grasses soon grow in and alongside beaver ponds. These plants are also favorite beaver snacks.

A Home High and Dry

Once their dam has created a pond, it's time for the beavers to build their **lodge**. They start by piling up more branches, mud, and stones in the water. The animals turn this pile into a cozy home with two rooms. One room is used for drying off and eating, and the second is for sleeping. They pack the sleeping room with grass and wood shavings to help keep it warm and dry. Underwater doors let beavers come and go from their lodge.

Beavers stay safe from **predators** by living in homes surrounded by water. A family with two adult beavers and as many as six of their kits can stay safe inside the watery home.

Life at the Lodge

Once the beavers have created a pond and built their home, a meadow soon surrounds the water. The grassy area is quickly filled with plant and animal life.

Insects find shelter and a place to lay their eggs in this new wetland. In turn, these insects are food for the fish that feel at home in the calm pond water. Around the water and even on top of the lodge, birds nest and feed on the pond's insects and fish. All kinds of plant and animal life find food and shelter in and around the beaver pond and meadow.

Healthy ecosystems must have **biodiversity**. Many different kinds of living things are needed there to support one another. The wetlands built by beavers create homes for dozens of plant and animal species.

Water Warriors

Though the wetlands that beavers create change the surrounding environment, they are relatively stable themselves. Beaver dams, the ecosystems' soil, and the plant life in and around wetlands are all part of a system that keeps a healthy level of water in the wetlands.

Dams slow water enough to allow it to move throughout the wetland before more comes in. This prevents flooding while also giving the soil and plants time to soak up water. Healthy, watered plants and slow-moving water keep the soil of the wetlands in place, preventing **erosion**.

In addition to helping prevent floods, beaver pond wetlands lessen the impact of **droughts**. Stored water can help plants when there is little rainfall.

Keeping It Clean

The water that makes its way through beaver ponds is also often healthier. In fast-moving rivers, **nutrients** found in dirt and mud get washed downstream. But when rivers and streams are dammed by beavers, the nutrients sink and settle at the pond's bottom. If **pollutants** wash into beaver ponds, the water is ready to get cleaning. The nutrients that have settled to the bottom of the pond filter and break down these pollutants, keeping the water clean for nearby plant and animal life.

Pollutants can wash into water from nearby farms and roadways.

Ponds created by beavers are so good at filtering pollutants that the water flowing out of the ponds is often cleaner than the water that flowed into them.

Here Comes the Sun!

Busy beavers are never done working, which directly benefits their wetland ecosystems. Even after they first build their dams and lodges, the furry creatures continue to chop down trees to add to and repair their woody creations.

When beavers take down old or dying trees, more sunlight is able to reach the ground to help seeds sprout. New, healthy plants and trees begin to grow to replace the ones that have been cut down. In this way, beavers act like gardeners, clearing out old and dying plant life. The marshy meadow around the pond bursts with life.

Each adult beaver can cut down hundreds of trees per year! It eats some of these plants and builds with the rest of them.

Beaver front teeth never stop growing. However, eating through tough plants keeps them trimmed.

That's Cool

Wetland ecosystems built by beavers provide a home and food for many kinds of life. But far from the water, these wetlands are helping life in other ways, too.

We burn **fossil fuels** to power our cars, homes, and businesses. Every time we do, we release a gas called **carbon dioxide** that traps heat around Earth and causes temperatures to rise. This extra warmth is changing our **climate** and causing unusual weather, monster storms, and severe droughts. But the plants and trees that grow in the wetlands **absorb** heat-trapping carbon dioxide. They clean the air of pollutants, just as nutrients in the ponds clean the water.

Wetlands can also help when wildfires start and spread as a result of climate change. The wet areas provide a natural barrier that may stop even the fiercest fires in their tracks.

1 The sun's light comes to Earth. Its heat warms the planet.

3 These gases keep extra heat around Earth.

2 Human activities send gases into the air.

4 Wetlands trap some carbon dioxide.

21

Beavers on the Brink

Beavers support our wetlands, but we have not always supported beavers. Fur **trappers** once hunted the animals almost to **extinction** in North America and Europe. Even after that practice stopped, some people continued to kill beavers because they believed the animals could cause flooding on their land. Others removed beaver dams and drained wetlands to make room for farms, homes, and businesses.

In the 1500s, there were as many as 400 million beavers in North America. By the beginning of the 20th century, fewer than 100,000 remained.

When beavers were killed or their homes destroyed, the ponds and meadows they created soon failed. The ecosystems couldn't continue without their keystone species.

Fur trappers would set up traps that sprung closed on beavers, keeping them in place.

Bye-Bye, Wetlands

Without beavers to maintain and repair it, a dam that once held back a river or stream may eventually fail. The resulting flood can have deadly consequences for life and property downstream. It often also washes away the nutrients in the beaver pond and causes erosion along the shoreline.

Eventually, a wetland without the dam dries out. The plants that need all that water die, and the animals that live in the slow-moving pond may not be able to survive in the flowing stream. An entire ecosystem of life can be lost.

Without beavers, an ecosystem's biodiversity decreases greatly. Some animals leave. Those that cannot make the move start to suffer in their new, unhealthy ecosystems.

When beaver dams fail, the water they were holding back comes rushing downstream all at once.

Turning the Tide

After seeing what happened to wetlands without their keystone species, some people took action. It is now illegal in many places to hunt beavers or to damage their dams and lodges. People are learning how to protect their property without killing the creatures.

Beavers are nature's builders. They create healthy ecosystems that are home to many plants and animals. In addition, the busy beavers' work leaves us with cleaner water, fresher air, and a cooler planet. Beavers truly are key!

Since protections have increased, beaver populations have rebounded. Today, there are as many as 15 million beavers living—and working—in North America.

Save the Beavers

Because beavers are so important to the health and well-being of life on our planet, when they are in danger, we all are. Luckily, there are some easy things we can do to protect this keystone species and help it in its life-giving work.

Spread the word about how beavers are a keystone species and why they must be protected.

If you see a beaver, a beaver dam, or a beaver lodge, leave it alone. Let the beaver go about its business building an ecosystem.

Write letters or emails to your local leaders about why it is important to make beaver hunting and trapping illegal and to protect wetlands.

Organize a group of friends and family to help clean up waterways and wetlands. Pick up trash that litters beaver ponds and meadows.

If you live near a lake or pond, be careful what you put on your yard or in your garden. Chemicals that kill bugs and help your lawn grow may also be bad for beavers and their ponds.

Glossary

absorb to take in or soak up

algae tiny plantlike living things often found in water

biodiversity the existence of many different kinds of plants and animals in an environment

carbon dioxide a greenhouse gas given off when fossil fuels are burned

climate the usual, expected weather in a place

dams walls or barriers built to hold back water

droughts long periods of time during which there is very little or no rain

ecosystem a community of animals and plants that depend on one another to live

endangered close to dying off completely

erosion the wearing away of rocks and soil by natural forces, such as water and wind

extinction when a type of plant or animal dies out completely

fossil fuels energy sources made from the remains of plants and animals that died millions of years ago

lodge a beaver's home

nutrients vitamins, minerals, and other substances needed by living things for health and growth

pollutants things that make the environment unclean and unhealthy

predators animals that hunt and eat other animals

species groups that plants and animals are divided into, according to similar characteristics

trappers people who catch wild animals

wetland an area of land where the soil is usually covered by shallow water

Read More

Backhouse, Frances. *Beavers: Radical Rodents and Ecosystem Engineers (Orca Wild).* Custer, WA: Orca Book Publishers, 2021.

Bergin, Raymond. *Wetland Life Connections (Life on Earth! Biodiversity Explained).* Minneapolis: Bearport Publishing Company, 2023.

Furstinger, Nancy. *Beaver Dams (Nature's Engineers).* New York: Weigl, 2020.

Learn More Online

1. Go to **www.factsurfer.com** or scan the QR code below.

2. Enter "**Keystone Beavers**" into the search box.

3. Click on the cover of this book to see a list of websites.

Index

About the Author

Della O'Dowd is a writer with a passion for nature. When she's not writing, she's hiking, drawing, or going on an adventure with her dog. It's her dream to visit every national park someday.